DATE DUE

PRINTED IN U.S.A.

SERVING OUR
COUNTRY

U.S. MARINES

by Rachel Grack

AMICUS | AMICUS INK

Amicus High Interest is published by Amicus and Amicus Ink
P.O. Box 1329, Mankato, MN 56002
www.amicuspublishing.us

Library of Congress Cataloging-in-Publication Data
Names: Koestler-Grack, Rachel A., 1973- author.
Title: U.S. Marines / by Rachel Grack.
Description: Mankato, Minnesota : Amicus, [2019] | Series: Serving our
 country | Includes index. | Audience: Grades K-3.
Identifiers: LCCN 2018002189 (print) | LCCN 2018002883 (ebook) | ISBN
 9781681516011 (pdf) | ISBN 9781681515632 (library binding)| ISBN
 9781681524016 (pbk.)
Subjects: LCSH: United States. Marine Corps--Juvenile literature. |
 Marines--United States--Juvenile literature.
Classification: LCC VE23 (ebook) | LCC VE23 .K67 2019 (print) | DDC
 359.9/60973--dc23
LC record available at https://lccn.loc.gov/2018002189

Photo Credits: DVIDS/Pfc. William Chockey cover; Shutterstock/Nikola
m background pattern; Marines website/MCRC 2; DVIDS/U.S. Marine
Corps photo by Cpl. Krista James/Released 4–5; Wikicommons/Official
U.S. Navy Photograph, National Archives 7; DOD/Marine photo 8–9;
DVIDS/U.S. Navy photo by Mass Communication Specialist 3rd Class
Reymundo A. Villegas III/Released 11; DVIDS/Cpl Sullivan Laramie 12–13;
DVIDS/DOD Flickr/Sgt. David Bickel 14–15; DVIDS/Cpl Meghan Gonzales
16; Marines website/LCpl. Chris Kutlesa 19;
DVIDS/Sgt Eric Wilterdink 20–21; Marines
Flickr/U.S. Marine Corps photo by Cpl.
Bobby J. Gonzalez 22

Editor: Wendy Dieker
Designer: Aubrey Harper
Photo Researcher: Holly Young

Printed in China

HC 10 9 8 7 6 5 4 3 2 1
PB 10 9 8 7 6 5 4 3 2 1

TABLE OF CONTENTS

MEET THE U.S. MARINES

America faces sudden danger! Who are the first to help? The U.S. Marines! They are highly trained. They move quickly in times of trouble. Marines come by land, sea, and air.

EARLY MARINES

The Marines began in the **Revolutionary War** (1775–83). They sailed to sea to fight. They protected the shore. In 1798, they became part of the new U.S. armed forces. Marines have fought in every U.S. war.

Force Fact
The Marines were formed to fight pirates on the high seas.

7

CHOSEN FORCE

The Marines are ready to go quickly. They are often first into battle. As part of the U.S. Navy, Marines protect the Navy's ships and bases. But they also help other **branches**. They are the chosen force.

FROM SEA TO LAND

Marines carry out **amphibious landings**. They can go on both water and land. A U.S. ship anchors off the coast. The enemy hides on land. Marines drive **AAVs** across the water and onto the beach. Attack!

Force Fact
An AAV is like a tank that floats on the water. Then it drives onto the land.

FIGHTING TO WIN

Marines train hard. They can overcome the worst. A cold wind blows. Marines march over snowy hills. Suddenly, the enemy surrounds them. They are outnumbered! Marines fight to win. They never give up.

IN THE AIR

Marines have missions from the sky. Armed helicopters lift off. It is still dark. They fly over the desert. Marines fire down at enemy troops. They destroy enemy forts.

HELPING IN TIMES OF TROUBLE

An earthquake shakes the ground! Buildings cave in. People need food and water. They need medical care. The U.S. Marines go at once. They are organized. They are skilled. They help people all over the world when **disasters** hit.

SERVING CHILDREN

The Marines work to make
the world a better place.
They helped build schools in
Honduras. They also started Toys
for Tots in the U.S. This program
brings holiday gifts to children
in need.

ALWAYS FAITHFUL

The **motto** of the U.S. Marines is "Always faithful." They will do anything for their country. They are there in times of trouble. They give their all on every front!

U.S. MARINES FAST FACTS

Founded: 1798

Members called: Marines

Main duties: To protect U.S. Navy ships and carry out immediate action for land, sea, and air missions.

Members on active duty: 180,000

Motto: "Semper fidelis" (Always faithful)

WORDS TO KNOW

AAVs Assault Amphibious Vehicles; armed vehicles used to go from boat to shore.

amphibious landing A type of attack that moves from water to land or land to water.

branch A group within a larger organization; the U.S. military branches are the Army, Navy, Marines, Air Force, and Coast Guard.

disasters Events that cause people great harm and loss.

motto A saying that tells what a group stands for or believes.

Revolutionary War The American war for independence fought between the American colonies and Great Britain from 1775 to 1783.

LEARN MORE

Books

Marx, Mandy R. *Amazing U.S. Marine Facts*. North Mankato, Minn.: Capstone Press, 2017.

Reed, Jennifer. *The U.S. Marine Corps*. North Mankato, Minn.: Capstone Press, 2017.

Sherman, Jill. *U.S. Navy*. Mankato, Minn.: Amicus, 2019.

Websites

Britannica Kids: Marines
https://kids.britannica.com/kids/article/marines/353430

Marine Corps | Approach, Purpose, & Mission
https://www.marines.com/who-we-are/our-purpose.html

INDEX